Who You Are, is a Fact

Someone Else's Perception of You is Merely an Opinion

By Kylee Blehm

Table of Contents

Dedication

To my grandmother, my mother and her sisters, each one of you have had a hand in everything I've written in this book, as you have shaped me into the woman I am today. Thank you for the inspiring and believing in me. To Taylor Gorton, I wish I could explain the influence you've had on my life. Thank you for bringing out the best version of myself, you are one of the reasons I found the courage to share this message. To Amber Skelton, I can never repay you for the things you've done for me when I needed it most, there are special jewels on your crown in heaven. To Lexi Nicholson, your light burns so bright, you've shown me love, support, forgiveness & the greatest of them all, Jesus. To Kylie Pethoud, thank you for always answering when I call, you've taught me so many lessons, I can never replace what you mean to me. Through all of the laughs and lessons, I appreciate and love you all the most.

-Kylee

Introduction

I have that same feeling you get right before you go on a first date. Butterflies and sweaty palms. Excited because this could grow into a beautiful relationship and nervous because you could be like my last first date, so drunk you pass out cold in the middle of dinner (true story, ill save it for my next book). Anyways, I've thought about you a lot while I wrote this book because most of these stories and experiences I've never shared before, even with close friends and family. About four months before I started writing, a friend of mine told me, "Kylee, you are doing the world and yourself a disservice by not sharing with them who you really are." Maybe that explains why my dates pass out? Either way I want you to be as vulnerable with yourself as I am with you as you live through my stories, grow through my mistakes and learn from my lessons.

You could say were kind of moving fast here because we are entering a full-on relationship in the next few minutes, and let's be honest, those are messy. Really, my words could be interpreted any way you want them to and I could pay consequences for sharing my truth and giving you my heart. So with that being said, I don't want you to guess at my intentions, I want you to laugh, cry and be moved as deeply as I have been and after all of that if you don't agree with what I've said I want you to at least know that I am honest. It's pretty scary to put myself out here like this; it makes me think I'm showing up to this date naked with no make-up on. As terrifying as this all is, this is my most authentic approach at giving you my true self, something I won't apologize for, in hopes that you will do the same in your life. So, if this dating profile seems appealing enough, go ahead and pour yourself a drink and swipe right. Chances are we've already matched.

Chapter 1

It Had to Happen

I had "my day" back in 2014; it was really like "my year" because this lasted far longer than a day. I was a senior in high school in a small town in Oklahoma. I was involved in all kinds of clubs, played sports year round, was well known around the community, in other words you could say I was one of the popular kids. Basketball being my favorite sport I had nearly wrapped my identity in it. I never put a ball down, I was in the gym always. I lead the team in scoring and rebounds and I traveled around the U.S. playing during the summer. It consumed my life until one day. My day, October 14th, I was asked to come to the principal's office for a meeting where they sat me down by myself, locked the office door, shut the blinds and told me another student led them to believe I was having an affair with a teacher at the school. You want to talk about earth shattering for a 17 year old? My world collapsed. Over the next few months, bad got worse. As the police interrogated me three times there was no way to keep this out of the public eye. Other students threatened to fight me, all of my friends but one turned their back on me, kids from other towns called & texted me to ask if "it really happened". The stress was so monumental one day that I barely made it to the bathroom before I profusely vomited. My character, reputation, everything I had built for myself was tarnished at the hand of someone else. On December 23rd I was finishing up my fourth investigation, this time with the OSBI and my story had already hit the news cycle. I genuinely thought there was nothing I could say or do to earn the respect of others for something that never happened. I couldn't see the light at the end of the tunnel. I thought this was who I will always be seen as. It was on this day that I thought my life was better lost than alive. Someone else's account of who I was and what they thought about me nearly put me 6 feet under. I wrote my letters and planned my escape; I was secretly hoping it wouldn't work. I didn't actually want to take my own life, all I really wanted was for this season to be over. It was then God spoke to me and showed me who I actually was.

I wrote in my journal, "I want to go home but I don't know where home is. I'm still suffering at night a lot, lately I haven't been getting much sleep. Sometimes I lay here in bed and close my eyes but tell myself not to fall asleep so I don't have to face tomorrow."

I was afraid I wouldn't go to heaven if I took my own life. I was afraid what it might do to my family that loved me and believed in me and for my future husband and children that God intended for me. As I contemplated my next steps, I found an article online written by an angel. They shared their feelings of being suicidal and for the first time in months, it felt like I had someone I could relate to. Not only did they share how they felt but they shared how they overcame their battle. A resource & lesson I will use for the rest of my life, they taught me to take one minute at a time. If I could just make it to the next minute, things would slowly get better, so that's what I did. My goal was to make it one more minute, until minutes turned into hours, hours into days and days into weeks. It was in this time I learned some of the most valuable lessons in my life, I just didn't know it yet.

A year after our investigation was closed and both of our innocence was proven, I was still depressed and genuinely traumatized. Every time the phone rang and I didn't recognize the number, my stomach sank as I thought it might be someone calling about the investigation. When someone would knock on our door, I got chill bumps thinking they might be here to question me. My nerves were shot and my heart was broken. It took a lot of therapy to wrap my head around the fact that this was not my identity, that it was merely a season of my life, something that had to happen.

I share my story of triumph, overcoming & healing because I know someone somewhere needs to hear why they have a purpose in this life. You might not have had "your day" yet and your day might not look anything like mine did but at some point in your life, your character will be questioned, and your confidence will be lowered and you need to know this beforehand so you don't have to suffer as long as I did. If you have reason to put your confidence in someone else's flesh I need you to know:

Who you are is a fact; someone else's perception of you is merely an opinion.

If you could see the person God has called you to be you wouldn't question the circumstances he has put in front of you. Your calling is *too high*, your character is *too great* and your purpose is *too significant* to give up before you have even started. If I would've given up on that day I wouldn't be here to appreciate everything life has to offer. We have 86,400 seconds given to us every single day and the freedom to choose how we spend them. If it were money, we would empty our accounts knowing we could always make more. Unlike money, you can't get time back. Because of that, I offer my time and my story so you don't waste yours. Whether you have a story or not, you have the incredible gift of time given to you free of charge but with no possible return. Spend your time finding success and building significance. The most important things in your life aren't for someone else to dictate, like your character and reputation. After this season of my life I learned that my purpose is not just one thing and it's definitely not just about me. God is using yours and my life for a greater purpose than we can imagine. If you believe you have missed your calling or fallen short of what you want in life you need to know and understand that your life is full of opportunity but it is up to you and only you to make it happen. Your blueprint isn't going to look that same as mine or anyone else's for that matter, meaning you have a unique opportunity to make your dreams come true at the *time* they were meant to for you. Don't look forward to your next month but step into your next minute.

"When you do not know what your next step should be sit down, close your eyes and quite your mind. Your intuition is ready to show you the way." –Nidhi Kush Shah

The irony about time is that it always keeps ticking whether you use it or not.

Chapter 2

When Purpose Knocks, You Answer

I've had quite a few jobs in my time, as I haven't stuck with any of them for longer than a few months. Pretty typical for a teenager or college age kid to bounce around jobs as their schedule changes and that's exactly what I did. It wasn't until I obtained my esthetics license that I had that job for over a year. When I hit that year mark it was a pretty big feat for me. I really felt like I had proven to myself that I could stay committed to one thing for more than a few months. It was in this time I had also learned my purpose.

I started my esthetics business knowing I loved helping clients with their skin but I really loved that I built intimate relationships with them. They sought after my advice with personal problems in their lives and I felt such a sense of gratitude. I was able to give them a fresh perspective and to me that was worth more than money. Half way in to my first year as an esthetician I launched my athletic wear line, practically by accident. I had been looking for a side hustle for fun and I saw an opportunity in the athlesiure wear market. As I was searching for lines to carry I submitted my info to what I thought was an athletic wear line. Come to find out, it was an athletic wear manufacturer. I almost hung up the phone when he told me I had to design my own line, after all I was no designer & I thought that definitely would require a degree of some sort—which I didn't have considering I dropped out of college. After I heard what he had to say I called three of my friends to ask what they thought and their responses were all similar, "Don't do it Kylee, there's already too many lines, what is going to make yours different?" I was furious as I argued with them over an answer to a question I didn't quite have yet. I couldn't understand why they didn't see what I saw; I was offended that they didn't think I was capable. The irony about being offended when someone doesn't think you are capable of doing something is because you are asking the wrong person. If this is you and your dream is on the line I'm going to need you to highlight this, do not let small minds convince you that your dreams are too big, quit asking society for validation, start asking yourself. Only you know what's inside of you.

Twenty-four hours after I came up with the idea, I started the design process and two very short months after that Beyond Athletica was born. I had no plan, I had no influence, just a vision and a solution to a problem within women's athletic wear that I wanted to do my part in fixing. Being that my company started completely online I wanted some sort of personal connection to be made. I felt like the best way to do that was to write to each of my customers when they made a purchase. I'm not talking about a typical "thank you for your purchase" letter, but a genuine, "You represent beyond so well, we are so thankful for you, wishing you and your family the best." letter. Customer by customer I hand wrote each of them, asking about their families, school, jobs, etc. My favorite part of packaging is knowing that I have the opportunity to tell them how much I appreciate them and how important they are to me. After years of what felt like searching for my purpose, it became obvious to me. I don't work in the retail business—I work in the people business. I created a product that is affordable, that fits every body type and most importantly makes you feel your best. The thing that fills me up, overflows my cup, is serving others. Through that I have learned that living a successful life is not yours or my purpose. Living a significant life is. If you put *meaning* into everything you do, you will find your purpose.

"If you can't figure out your purpose, figure out your passion. For your passion will lead you right into your purpose." – TD Jakes

At first, this was challenging because I didn't understand how to make everything meaningful. What I did understand was how to be empathetic. I put myself in the customer's shoes and asked, "If they did this for me how would I feel because of it?" It made finding a purpose for how I spend my time and my actions relatable and people responded because of it.

I can't tell you where you will find your purpose because it will look different than mine and to be honest finding your purpose isn't the goal, living your purpose is what life is all about. I don't believe that you were set out to be one thing and one identity, as my purpose will change as my life does. I believe you were put on this earth with multiple talents & aspirations, some bigger and better than others and it's up to you to put meaning into them. The difference between the version of who you are today and who you will be tomorrow is how willing you are to get there.

Growth and potential don't happen overnight, they're intentional. I really wish it was that easy, to wake up and understand why you are who you are and what God put you on this earth to do, but I'd be lying to you if I told you that will just happen one day. I've witnessed far too many people search for purpose their entire lives and come up empty handed because they didn't understand that to find purpose they had to first put purpose into everything that they are doing. You will find it and it will be bigger and greater than you ever expected it to be and that's because it's hidden in a place you've never thought to look before. It's all around you, you experience it everyday but you have yet to open your eyes to the possibility. I know this because I nearly missed it. My focus was set on carrying someone else's brand because that is all I thought I was capable of. If I hadn't been open to the possibility that I could design something and succeed it would've taken me a lot longer to figure out what I was passionate about.

Because I have learned this I've never had as much gratitude as I do now. When I intentionally tell someone how I feel and pay them a compliment, it's a part of who I am. I care now more about the genuine connection than I do about the sale. I also spend less time worrying about my future and more time dreaming and seeking my potential, all because I put meaning into everything I did.

As Maya Angelou said,
"I've learned that people will forget what you said, people will forget what you did, but people will never forget how you made them feel."

There are two qualities someone *living in* purpose possesses:

1. They have the ability to forgive themselves for their weaknesses and the humility to work on it.
2. They can reframe their outlook on any given situation and find the positive and focus on it. Not that they shut out other emotions but that

they give prevalence to what is most important and what will serve them in the long run.

I challenge you to forgive yourself for the thing that's holding you back from your purpose; we all have a barrier that is keeping us from pursing our passion. It's not a physical barrier but a mental block from the person you are and the person you want to be. Chances are you're letting your lack of resources, connections, competence and fear hold you back, when really those are small things on your list to figure out. Your perspective is what needs to change. If you really want a different result your willingness to succeed is what will get you there.

As Wayne Dyer says,
"If we change the way we look at things, the things we look at change."

Chapter 3

Look Through Your Insecurity

I'm supposed to love myself but how do I even do that?

That's what they tell you right? All of the self help books & motivational speakers. To just wake up and love the belly that hangs over your jeans and the stretch marks on your legs and the crooked teeth in your mouth. Just love it because it's you and you are the perfect version of yourself.

I never really understood that.

If that was the truth and I accepted those things about myself then why don't I *feel* like I love myself? Why do I still *question* if I am enough? Why do I still *want* to change?

Now-a-days you hear a lot about social media being the reason so many women are insecure about themselves and their body image, although I don't disagree, my body dismorphia started way before social media was even thought of. My younger brother and I are almost two years apart in age so growing up, we experienced a lot of the same things at the same time. He has always been a beanpole and when I was a little girl I definitely took notice of it. I remember wondering why he ate the same things I ate, played the same games I played, came from the same parents I came from but he had abs and my belly hung over my jeans.

When I was eight years old I went to him and asked what he did to stay in shape, he told me "I don't know Kylee, I work out?" I said, "Okay Cale, well I need you to be my trainer, I want to have abs like you." So he took me outside on scolding summers day and told me to do 100 sit-ups, he even brought a whistle to blow at me when I was slacking. We were serious about this ab game and he wasn't going to let me down. To our surprise doing 100 sit-ups didn't burn my "baby fat" and my tummy was still soft, we didn't give up though, I followed him around like a fly that day, making sure I ate what he ate, drank what he drank and exercised when he exercised. After 24 hours my childlike faith and patience were running out. I just knew my belly would hang forever and my biggest fear at the time would come true, I would be fat.

As an adult I think back to this time in my life and wonder why an 8-year-old would have this fear, where could this have come from?

You see, it didn't take cell phones and social media to compare myself to someone. It just took me noticing the difference between myself and someone else to start the vicious cycle of negative self-talk for the next 12 years.

When I was 18 years old I was given the opportunity to travel to Los Angeles and visit a few modeling agencies. I was stoked; I just knew this was the beginning of my modeling career. I got started preparing my body right away. I reached out to a friend, a former model in the LA industry and asked for diet advice, I needed to know the quickest way to tone up so I would for sure sign a contract. Because I've played sports my entire life the muscle tone in my legs and arms are pretty prevalent and not the kind agencies look for in a print or runway model. She decided the best thing that I could do was to start out only eating egg whites, veggies and some meat like fish or chicken and to walk for two hours a day. I wanted to give myself the best chance possible, to prove to myself for the first time that I could have the body that I always desired. I was crazy enough that when I knew I was traveling I packed an ice chest of food that I could eat and carried it with me, I got up as early or stayed out as late to finish my two hours of walking which usually equated to 8-10 miles a day. I even became so desperate I got my hands on prescription diet pills and water pills because I was starving and it took everything in me to control my urge to eat. After a month into my regimen I wasn't losing enough weight so I went to a liquid only diet. I was to eat a certain vegetable-based protein shake three times a day along with an apple, 8 miles was no longer enough and 10-12 was the minimum. I did it, day in and day out for another 30 days I carried my shakes in ice chests, walked for 3 hours till the lactic acid was unbearable and consumed on average 500 calories a day. My hair fell out, my skin was fragile and I went from a size 8 to a 2. The week had finally arrived though, I had over 10 meetings set up with various agencies and nothing was going to hold me back. Meeting after meeting all week long I heard to same two things, 1. We already have someone that looks like you OR 2. Your measurements do not fit our criteria.

I was truly elated, thank you God I do not meet their standards.

Not the response you expected considering how hard I worked to get to those meetings but I realized something as I was there.

I cannot survive treating my body and myself obtaining their standards and that is not the kind of life I wanted to live.

After all of that work and rollercoaster of emotion you would think I had a new appreciation for my body, after all, I put it through some extreme circumstances but I didn't, I still didn't love my body any differently at a one-hundred and thirty pounds than one hundred and fifty and so the negative self-talk still continued.

When I signed up for my first pageant I knew very little about what I was getting myself into and I knew even less about the person I would become because of it. What I did know is that a portion of the competition was swimsuit and that really made me nauseous. If you scroll through my camera roll you'll find a lot of "before" pictures in bathing suits, you know, the ones you plan on following up with an after picture where you can see your six pack abs and toned up legs? I have yet to accomplish such a thing in my life so, for now, I have a slideshow of befores.

I've always had a vision of what I wanted my body to look like and I'm pretty sure that vision would require my torso to be about an inch longer than what it is naturally and my genetics to come from a different gene pool. I obviously knew the picture in my head wasn't possible so before I let myself walk out in front of a crowd and judging panel I made two promises to myself:

1.   To not treat my body that way I had previously

2.   To overcome my insecurity before I walked on stage.

With only two and a half months away from the pageant I wanted to do things the right way. I hired a personal trainer and nutritionist and worked with them daily. I learned the correct way to lift weights, the right amount of cardio for my body and the proper daily calorie intake. Very shortly my body was starting to change, I was looking more tone, I was feeling better, my hair wasn't falling out and my skin was glowing. Everything on the outside was coming together but the way I felt on the inside wasn't. The closer the pageant got the more pressure I felt, until one day after 13 years I couldn't stand it anymore. My mom and I were practicing my catwalk in a studio, surrounded by mirrors, my chest tight, my stomach in knots, I couldn't even stand to look at myself because I was too afraid to see in the mirror what I felt inside. On the inside I felt like the button on my jeans would pop if I didn't keep my stomach sucked in, I couldn't stand the thought of my belly hanging over my jeans or the way my arm fat rested on the side of my body, the vision I had in my head was taking consumed me until I broke.

Broken & sobbing I looked at my mom and asked her to leave, I knew this was my fork in the road, this insecurity was going to consume me or I was going to consume it. I picked my head up and looked in the mirror, I stripped down to just my bra and panties and stood there, the lights weren't dimmed, my body wasn't tan, and I had nothing to cover me. I said to myself, "okay Kylee, just do it, pick yourself apart because this is your last chance." With the most innocent look in my eyes, my mouth trembling, I wept.

I wept because I spent the last 13 years picking myself apart, telling myself I needed to do better when in reality I needed to open my eyes and define myself for what I really am, a strong, beautiful woman. I needed to look through my insecurity and so do you. I don't know what package you come wrapped in but I can tell you right now what you are holding on to, what's eating you up inside is not serving you and if it's not making you a better version of yourself it's not worth having.

Sister, you have to look through your insecurity, not around it, above or below it, look through it.

"You must win in your mind before you win in reality." – Simon Alexander Ong

And let me tell you, just because I was able to see myself for who I really was for the first time does not mean I didn't fall right back in those thoughts and feelings ALL THE TIME. I did & so will you but it doesn't belong there and so it doesn't stay there. I had to discipline my mind to react to each and every negative thought. A few weeks after this I was shopping for a bathing suit to wear in the pageant, as I was sending pictures of my options back and forth to my coach I was so ashamed at how I looked, devastated because I thought I had developed a new mantra. I walked out of the store with a bathing suit in hand and a heavy heart knowing there wasn't much I could do for my body in the next week before the pageant. I also knew I couldn't go in feeling like this, especially if I wanted to set an example for others and myself. Once again, another choice, do I let my insecurity consume me or do I consume it. In the car, out loud, in front of my mother I yelled, "Damn it, Kylee, if you wouldn't say someone else is fat why do you think it's okay to say that about yourself?"

The weight, the 100 pounds I felt lifted off of my chest in a matter of seconds. Not only did I understand my insecurity but I understood how to control it. Here is the truth about insecurities; they are always going to be there. You though have an option, you can let them serve you or you can serve them. And the coolest thing about changing my perspective is that the physical way I saw my body changed in that instant. What I had picked apart earlier was no longer there and it was the first time I saw my body for it's actual shape. I am so thankful that I put myself in the position to get over what I feared most. My pageant experience taught me that they aren't looking for a certain body type; they're looking for the woman that embodies her own body type. I am proud to say that two months later I graced the stage in little white bikini, heels, bright lights and a few thousand eyes looking only at me with the biggest smile on my face because I knew they were looking at the women I am; the confidently beautiful one.

I dare you, look through your insecurity, it's time you fight for yourself and the women that you already are, You will find that shifting your perspective doesn't mean you change your lifestyle immediately, it means that you discipline your mind to the only thoughts that serve you rather than one's that don't; When you start with your mind you will see yourself change physically, as well as have confidence in who you are and do it on purpose.

 If you are going to rise, you might as well shine.

Chapter 4

What it Means to Have Confidence

So what is confidence?

We respect people who have it, we find a reason to doubt it and we wish we had more of it.

Confidence

I believe that confidence is 'an act of', an act of performance, impulse, discipline, and knowledge. There have been studies that have shown that confidence is somewhat genetic, that some people are born with more confidence than others. Although that may be true I believe confidence is something that can be controlled. At some point in our lives, we've had to perform in some way or another, it could possibly be at a job, or you could be an athlete, or you could be giving a presentation in front of a class but in some way you have physically performed something in front of someone. Whether it came easy to you or not, at some point during that you had to have confidence in what you were doing, even if you didn't feel it, it was there.

Try to imagine a time in your life where you have told yourself you are capable of something you've never done before. For myself competing in my first pageant was as foreign to me as reading Chinese. As I explained earlier I had some insecurities to work through as well as multiple lessons to learn before I walked on stage, but I didn't give myself a choice at failing because failing was not trying. Think back to a time that you kept a promise to yourself. I didn't understand the importance of this until I read "Girl Wash Your Face" by Rachel Hollis where she really put it in perspective for me what I was doing to myself when I didn't follow through with the promises I made to myself, in turn shedding some light on the reasons why I felt guilty when this happened. Finally, I want you to think about a time you accomplished something just based off of knowledge. Let's be honest, I'm no scholar and when I was in college my first semester my GPA was a 2.5, it really reflected the effort I had put into my classes thus far. After being put on academic probation within my sorority and feeling guilty because I knew I could do better I spent the entire semester learning how to study, as this was my biggest problem. It really paid off for me when I finished with a strong 3.5 and showed myself I was capable of succeeding in an area I knew I struggled in. Performance, impulses, discipline, and knowledge all require action and all action requires confidence. All four of those things are within you, weaved into every fiber of your body. It is your job though to bring those things to the surface, but first, you must understand why you carry doubt baggage.

I'm going to assume you've never heard of doubt baggage... mainly because I made it up; not the concept, but the phrase. To put this into perspective I need you to picture this scenario for me: You wake up, take a look in the mirror, you're a woman.

Yep, that is why you have doubt baggage, you're a woman.

Unlike men, who sometimes doubt but rarely put more thought into it than that, women are wired to overthink. We think more about the future and what could happen. We think about the consequences of failure. We think about what decisions will impact our lives and how much it will change because of it. Don't take this as a negative though, this is why were mothers, why were caregivers, why we have compassionate hearts, why it takes us longer to make decisions. We look at both sides of the consequences.

If doubt isn't negative though, why do we have baggage?

Because we let the consequences of our decisions control our emotions.

Picture this, you're on the Miss USA stage answering the final question, your answer determines your outcome, you're asked a controversial question and you KNOW that your answer will either please the judges or not, so you go back and forth until your time is up, never really finding the confidence to say what you actually believe.

Imagine knowing that you were already the winner, that your answer to the question didn't determine the outcome. How would you have answered it? Confidently, of course, you are already the winner; you would have said what you actually believed. To make my point, as women, we underestimate our ability to achieve something because we consider every possible outcome before we act, discounting our potential, degrading our confidence and lowering our self-esteem.

Baggage.

I am a victim of this type of baggage, although I like to consider myself the culprit; It didn't happen 'to me,' it happened because 'of me'. Because of this, I spent a lot of time thinking about a complex way to fix this problem that almost every woman at some point faces. After a lot of hours and many methods, I finally found the one that worked. Are you ready for it? You might want to highlight this.

Simply spend less time thinking about the consequences of failure.

Yes, that simple fix. Simply spend less time thinking about all of the many ways you could fail.

True confidence is not a feeling, it's a fact, it's not something you have in every situation or area of your life, and it's a submission to doing things that you aren't exactly sure of over and over, failure or success to grow your confidence. I hope that you perform like there is no consequence to messing up, impulsively accomplish your goals before you have time to decide if they're good enough or not, discipline your mind and your body to keep going no matter the circumstances and educate yourself so you not only possess confidence but competence as well.

And even after all of that, there will still be instances where you doubt yourself so I want you to remember, it is okay to doubt yourself, but don't carry baggage with that doubt. You can control your confidence or it can control you.

"One important key to success is self-confidence. An important key to self-confidence is preparation."-Arthur Ashe

Chapter 5

An Inner Peace On The Other Side of Vulnerability

Like most little girls I've dreamt of my wedding day for years. I imagined every detail from the color of my bridesmaid dresses to the taste of my wedding cake, you name it, I have a Pinterest board for it. A vision of mine for a long time had been for my dad to stand up at my wedding, giving a toast to my family and friends about the little girl I once was and the women he has witnessed me grow into, handing me off to the man that will take care of me for the rest of my life, all the while shedding a tear and sharing his best-kept secrets of a long, meaningful marriage.

That dream was ruined when I was 13 years old. It was then that I realized my dad would never be "that dad" and my family would never be "that" family. My parents could no longer live together; my family could no longer be together. Because I was so young I didn't think it really mattered, I took the high road and looked forward to the positive side of a divorced family. I had no idea that I would carry that hopeless fantasy with me for 7 more years.

After the divorce, my dad seemed to become less and less prevalent in my life. I dreaded the weekends that I had to spend waiting on him to come home when he was supposed to be spending time with my siblings and I. I couldn't stomach the thought of another TV dinner or bowl of cereal to eat by myself instead of the home cooked meal around the table that I once had. But I especially hated feeling like I was there to spend time with my dad instead of my dad spending time with me. So I stopped trying, I quit going to his house as often, communication only happened on holidays and birthdays, acquaintances turned into hello's and goodbye's; A father and daughter turned into strangers. During this time relationships became more obvious to me, I watched my friends laugh and love with their fathers, I listened to men talk about how much they love their daughters, I held back tears as I dreamed what it must feel like to have that kind of relationship, I wanted that kind of love in my life, the kind of love you can only receive from your father. Seven years of building a fantasy in my head of what I missed out on, in the process becoming jaded.

Here's the thing about being jaded, you make that your identity...

For you, this might not be your relationship with your father, it could be the mother you've always wanted, the siblings you never talk to, the friendship that fizzled or even the job that you lost, the goal you never accomplished, the person you never became.

Sister, before you think that's not true let me put it in perspective for you.

Years passed and I "got over" the idea of the kind of father I wanted my dad to be, I use the quotations with that phrase because although I didn't cry every time I saw my friends and their dads share a moment, my heart was still hurt. The pain wasn't present but the past was.

Jaded.

To be able to write this chapter I had to understand this feeling, accept it and work on it.

So I will warn you, if you are 'jaded' this is just the start, as we peel back the layers of this I challenge you to be open and honest with yourself about how you really feel.

There is inner peace on the other side of vulnerability.

For me, being vulnerable meant talking about how I really felt, hearing myself, my thoughts, and my pain. At this point I had no desire to talk to my dad and explain these feelings so I did the next best thing, I wrote him a letter, a letter that he will never see. I don't know who this person is for you but I think you deserve to write them a letter. Before you start you need to know that you first have to be willing to forgive them. Forgiveness doesn't have to mean that you rekindle a relationship either; it just means that you are willing to let go of this pain for YOURSELF.

I want you to follow a format as you write this letter, it's going to cause you to think deep and communicate effectively. With every conversation you start at zero, you can either start with a positive or negative statement. Because so much is triggered as you do this exercise it's a natural reaction to want to start with a negative statement, but since we are trying to grow and heal I want you to start each point with 3 positive statements; value, love & appreciate. It went something like this for me:

Dad,

I value who you are on this earth, I love that you came to watch me in my pageant and I appreciate when you reach out to me.

Writing your positive statements might be the most difficult part of the exercise but it is the most crucial because it is here where you learn the most about yourself. I never thought there was anything I valued, loved or appreciated about my relationship with my dad but it revealed to me that I respect him as a human, I notice when he shows up and I realize when he reaches out. Because of these three things I was able to draw my boundary line. I knew how much my dad was willing to put into our relationship and I learned what I expected of him because of it. It was after, that I poured my heart out in my letter, I didn't run from my feelings, I let myself cry and my heart grieve.

When you can figure out the purpose of that relationship you can bring yourself 100% forward so that all of your other relationships don't pay for your last. Until you understand and are complete in these answers you seek them in the future. You find voids to fill, longing for what you think you missed out on. It's an overflow. It flows into more aspects of every relationship, men, women, friends, and family than you realize. You have to understand every relationship you encounter is purposeful. It's either a lesson learned or it's life-giving. It's your job to figure out which one and to figure out what it gave you.

And then

Move On Into Your Future

Forgiveness is not ignoring that it happened, it's not acknowledging that it didn't hurt you. Forgiveness is no longer living in resentment; don't choose to live in your pain when healing is an option.

"Resentment is like drinking poison and waiting
for the other person to die"
-Carrie Fisher

Someone is going to come into your life tomorrow, next week, next year that needs the love that you have to offer, someone needs who you are. And in order for you to be available, you need to have such an abundance of love and forgiveness that you are no longer taking away from yourself but offering them from your overflow. Your value isn't determined based on someone's inability to see your worth so please remember when you see this person again, they will still look the same, feel the same & even talk the same; it is in that moment you will realize what has changed is you.

Chapter 6

The World is Following the Lead of How You Treat Yourself

Being your best self, stepping into your purpose and following your dreams require each and every step I have talked about but if I'm really being honest none of that will change your life if you don't do this one last thing. It's kind of a secret though that I've learned from the most successful people I know. Before I tell you what it is I think it's important that we define success. Most would say success is a number in a bank account, a new initial to put after your name or a celebrity like status. Although those are admirable I don't believe that is the only definition of success. In my opinion, success comes only after you have failed. Being that I've always been an entrepreneur my first business venture was my freshman year of college, I wanted to open a clothing boutique with aspirations of a brick and mortar one day but I was scared, not that I would fail but I was scared of what people would think of me if I did fail. Because I wanted to do this so badly I didn't let that stop me from going through with it but I did let it stop me from succeeding at it. I started my clothing boutique, I built my website, I advertised, I filled orders, I took pictures, I bought new items yet you didn't know it was me and because it was inevitable to hide completely I told everyone I just know the owner and I help her out. It gave me peace of mind because I knew that to the public if it failed "the company" failed, Kylee didn't and so for the few months that I was opened I hid, behind the scenes, the orders, the pictures and the clothing hoping that my identity was not revealed. This probably doesn't shock you but because I allowed others opinions to dictate my choices it didn't take long for me to shut down after I listened to someone tell me that I would never succeed. As I reflect on that story a very humbling feeling comes over me as I can now say that I have opened the clothing store I've always dreamt about, in an even bigger and better way than I could've imagined but there is a BIG difference between the girl who cared too much and the women I am today and that's my secret. I watched, studied & talked to successful, happy people and figured out they all have one quality that is alike and the craziest thing about it is that every single one of us can possess this same quality. Every one of them does not let the idea that they may fail keep them from being their unapologetic self; who they are is a fact.

My world, my life & my perspective all changed when I when I stepped into my true self and did it on purpose; I defined failure. Failure to me didn't come wrapped in someone else's opinion anymore it came as the thought of holding myself back from success. It is the reason why I found the courage to write this book and share my message with the world and the confidence to open my first brick and mortar, the biggest personal success thus far in my life so I say with one thousand percent confidence and full transparency shifting your perspective will do the same for you.

Everyday I have a mental checklist and affirmation I read before I go anywhere.

1. What are my long, middle & short term goals
   a. 5 years
   b. 5 months
   c. 5 hours
2. What am I worrying about?

    a. Is there something I can do about it?

    b. Is it out of my control?

3. How can I make someone else's life better today?

    a. Pay a compliment

    b. Send someone a text/call

    c. Who can I pray for?

"My life is in the hands of the maker, I do things from a place of love and gratitude. I am strong and capable of incredible things. I have a servant heart and a calling to make a difference. I am no better than anyone else but I am just as good and my purpose is to give all of that away by being the best version of me today."

This checklist and daily affirmation allows me to keep my thoughts in proper prospective without losing sight of who I am, what I need to accomplish and my purpose.

Today and everyday really think about the desires of your heart and write them down, don't waste your time worrying on what you can't control and focus on what you can, keep your attention on your goals and stay steady, in other words, put your head down and do the work and always remember that you can impact someone else's life just by paying it forward with a simple message of gratitude. Lastly, the most valuable lessons that you can teach yourself is that you can create your own fire; quit waiting for the world to choose you, after all the world is following the lead of how you treat yourself. And finally, please remember one last thing, your ideas, visions, and goals don't make it out into the world unless you do first; who you are is a fact.